REPEAT AFTER ME;
I AM A
MILLIONAIRE
THE SECRET OF THE MILLIONAIRES

Copyright @ 2022 by Israel Joshua Chukwubueze

All rights reserved, no portion of this book may be reproduced, stored in a retrieval system, or transmitted in any form or by any means – electronic, mechanical, photocopy, recording, scanning, or other except for brief quotations in critical reviews or articles, without the prior written permission of the publisher.

This book may be purchased in bulk for educational, business, fundraising, or sales promotional use.

ISBN:

Published by: **Ekesy In-Outdoor Company**
10B, Mufutau Opeifa Street, Oke-Odo, Ile-Epo B/Stop, Alimosho, Lagos, Nigeria
Email: ekesygroup@gmail.com
Tel: 08038154459, 08132228534

Printed by: **Demrok Prints**

For information, please contact us @
ekesygroup@gmail.com
israeljoshua.com.ng
Call: 08064342968, 08038154459
WATSAPP: 08132228534

DEDICATION
This book is dedicated to my God, Mom, Kids, Friends, Colleagues, and my humble Staff.
And everyone who wish me well.

ISRAEL JOSHUA CHUKWUBUEZE

ACKNOWLEDGEMENT

I owe special thanks to several people who made it possible for me to complete this book in the face of challenges and several tight responsibilities.

And thanks to my mom, who have always helped me in taking care of my kids; the love is beyond words.

And to my kids, who understand about the many nights and weekends that I have spent working on this book; I appreciate your patience.

And to God, may all glory be to Him.

FOREWORD

Wealth has to remain arguably one of the essential ingredients in living; without money, one cannot attain a certain societal height or even survive. Wealth is everything that everyone needs to live life, comfortably or sustainably. We can argue other things, but money controls virtually everything.

This book envisaged the ways one can acquire wealth legitimately and smartly. With the introduction of technology, young men and women are taking the opportunity to learn things that will advance their knowledge also, expose them to new opportunities and that's what this book has been able to achieve by ensuring the right tools are being used in the right ways to acquire wealth. This isn't another book that's entered to motivate people, no, this isn't another acquire to perspire to aspire – this is in real-time, the real deal to make money legitimately and smartly.

The author is a good friend of mine and we've known each other for a period of more than five years, and I can affirm and attest that his great wealth of experience in financial literacy and liberation is indubitably rich. He has outlined information with experiences and also, practically, put that information in a way it will be made easy for anyone seeking financial freedom.

Reading this book, "REPEAT AFTER ME; I AM A MILLIONAIRE" I know for sure, there are going to be lots of testimonies.

Happy reading!

~**Chidibere A. Okoroji,** *M.Ed*

PREFACE

This book is written to impact knowledge on financial freedom and liberation, especially during this period of economic challenges. I have been able to outline perfect solutions that will enable readers to have practical ideas on wealth creation using the "REPEAT AFTER ME; I AM A MILLIONAIRE" as a guide.

I'm the MD/CEO of Ekesy In-Outdoor Company with brand services like eWeb9ja.com, 24000hosting.com, MamaEkene.com, and israeljoshua.com.ng.

You can browse online to confirm my claims for authentication. My official name is Christopher Ekene Okade (now Israel Joshua Chukwubueze).

This book is a collection of what I do, that changes the story of my life. Life can be more complex and you need to have a road map to get to your destination faster and easier.
Success and happiness require great and smart work; failure and struggling require no effort but, which one of them will you choose? I choose great and smart work because I know for sure that the rewards are great.

I will recommend this book to those who want to create wealth and be successful and comfortable.
The book is loaded with information on life experiences, exposure, knowledge, and other study references from successful men and women. This book will improve and change your mind

on our wealth and wealth creation.

~Israel Joshua Chukwubueze

TABLE OF CONTENTS
i.   Cover Page
ii. Title and Copyright
iii. Dedication
iv. Acknowledgement
v.   Foreword
vi. Preface
vii. INTRODUCTION

CHAPTER ONE
LET'S DO THE MATHS

CHAPTER TWO
DESIRE TO BE A MILLIONAIRE

CHAPTER THREE
YOUR BELIEF SYSTEM

CHAPTER FOUR
DREAM AND ACT BIG

CHAPTER FIVE
THE PRIZE OF SUCCESS

CHAPTER SIX
VALUE

CHAPTER SEVEN
SKILLS

CHAPTER EIGHT
ABILITY TO SELL

CHAPTER NINE
CONTACTS AND NETWORKS

CHAPTER TEN
TWO-EDGED SWORD THAT BREAKS YOU THROUGH ONLINE SUCCESS

CHAPTER ELEVEN
YOU NEED MONEY TO MAKE MORE MONEY

CHAPTER TWELVE
HOW I MAKE 1,095,000 (MILLION) IN ONE YEAR

INTRODUCTION

I'm a Millionaire

Most people don't think or believe that they can be a millionaire. Most people also don't know how to be a millionaire, others don't ever desire to be one, while some wish that one day, they will miraculously become a millionaire.

The truth is that you can be a millionaire but first you must believe and desire to be a millionaire, trust me, there are two things that are holding you back.

First, is Knowledge; you don't most likely have knowledge of how you don't somehow know the full details or knowledge about how to be a millionaire.

Secondly, somehow you have some knowledge but you never make a plan and take the action to become a millionaire.

In this book, you will learn some truth/knowledge about how to be a millionaire and this book will provide you with some planned actions you need to take through your journey into your rich and wealth creation to become the millionaire that your heart desired.

CHAPTER 1

LET DO THE MATHS

To become a millionaire becomes simple if you understand the maths.

Millionaires and billionaires are about numbers, that is the simplest breakdown I can give you. But let go deeper into the Millionaire Maths.

To be a millionaire, which is about numbers, all you need to do, is to Earn these numbers; the question is now how?

VALUE + EXCHANGE = EARNERS

Now let me explain what I mean above.

To become a millionaire or earn the millionaire numbers, you need to have a value that you can use to exchange for money.

The next question now is:
- What is a Value?
- What is an Exchange?
- Whom are we exchanging with?

Value can simply mean a Product or Service that you can offer to someone that can add value to their life.

That is, if you can find or create a product or service that someone can use, that will enhance or improve the quality of their life.

Exchange is a process where you give value to someone and someone gives you their money in exchange for the value (product or service) you offer them.

How do you become a millionaire?

If being a millionaire is about numbers, let's even go deeper into millionaire maths.

Find or create a product or service that lots of people want and offer them the product or service in exchange for their money.

VALUE (Product or Service) ($)	+	EXCHANGE (with People money)	=	EARNING (Profits in Millions)
5	+	200,000	=	1,000,000
10	+	100,000	=	1,000,000
20	+	50,000	=	1,000,000
50	+	20,000	=	1,000,000
100	+	10,000	=	1,000,000
500	+	2,000	=	1,000,000
1,000	+	1,000	=	1,000,000
5,000	+	200	=	1,000,000
10,000	+	100	=	1,000,000
50,000	+	20	=	1,000,000
100,000	+	10	=	1,000,000

From the above-sampled numbers, you will discover that, if you can find or create a product or service that can add value to lots of people's lives, they will give you their money in exchange for the value you are offering them.

So, the higher the worth of value you are offering, the lower the number of people you need to find to exchange their money for your value.

It's easier to exchange or sell lower value worth than the higher value worth, but more work is required to find more people t exchange or sell it to.

It's harder to exchange or sell higher value worth than the lower value worth, but less work is required to find fewer people t exchange or sell it to.

CHAPTER TWO
DESIRE TO BE A MILLIONAIRE

Most people never desire to be a millionaire, while some think that that financial level is not for them, some are even afraid to be one.

Desire is the beginning of every ambition, there is nothing wrong in being rich or being a millionaire. Well, if somehow you believe that money is the root of evil, this might be what is holding you back, to have the desire of becoming rich is the first step needed to become rich and wealthy.

Money is not the root of evil, but the love of money.
The thing about the good things you can do with money.
First, you can change the property history of your family, you can create jobs and help the less privileged, you can travel the world, and you can go to London to see the King (after the death of Queen Elizabeth II).

So nothing is bad or evil about money, but the things you do with money are what matters.

So Desire to become a millionaire, and when you become one, promised yourself that you will do good and only good things with the money.

CHAPTER THREE
YOUR BELIEVE SYSTEM

Most people don't believe that they can ever become rich or become a millionaire, to some of them, it never occurs to them that in their lifetime, they can acquire that can of wealth.

Your belief system is everything, your belief system can make you or break you.
The level of your belief is in relationship with the level of your growth and success in life.

Whatever you believe consciously or unconsciously will be after your life, whether you like it or not.

The question you are going to ask yourself now is; I'm a millionaire right now?
If your answer is No, then check your belief about riches or wealth.

If you are not a million or if you are poor, this means somewhere in your mind, something is happening in there, maybe:
1. you don't believe that you can be a millionaire.
2. it never occurs to you that you can be a millionaire.
3. somehow you believe that rich and wealthy people are evil people.
4. or you somehow believe that being rich will not allow you to make heaven, etc.

So to change everything about your financial life, you must change your belief, you must change your mindset about money, and acquire wealth, you must strongly believe that you can become successful and rich.

Faith cometh by hearing, reading this book, and meditating about the book day and night, reading a practicing what you read in this book will help you change your beliefs and mindset.

CHAPTER FOUR
DREAM AND ACT BIG

Most people don't dream at all, some dream small and are afraid of dreaming, you can't be a millionaire, if you don't dream to be a millionaire, so dream big and dream to be a millionaire.

Dreaming is free, great people are people who dream big, people who can see beyond what ordinary eyes can see, and people who can dream into the future, you don't pay anything for dreaming, no price to dream, so dream big as you want.

All successful people, millionaires, and billionaires dream big, the bigger your dream is, the bigger the millions and billions you can acquire.

Imagine coming from a poor family, and one day, you announce to them that you want to be a millionaire, most people will think you are crazy, yes, dreamers are something called crazy people until they surprise them by proving them wrong.

So don't worry, when people who can't into your dreams think you are crazy, just go to work, and prove them wrong.

Bill Gate, Elon Most, Donald Trump, Mark Zuckerberg, Dangote, Femi Otedola, etc, dreams big and bigger, which is why they're able to acquire these bigger amount of money in millions and billions.

So many people dream big but the downfall is that so many people is that after dreaming big, they fail to act big.

After finishing reading this book, if you fail to Act Big, you will not achieve much, so don't let that person be you.

When you dream big, take the next step by Acting big.

Don't let the work Act Big scare you, to act big, you must first plan out your strategies, break down your big dream into smaller achievable steps, and take a step one after the other.

A journey of One Thousand Mile begins with One Step after the other.
To build a giant brick wall, you have to lay One Brick at a time.

So Dream Big, Act Big, Plan, and Strategics your Big Dreams into Smaller Actionable steps, and take at least one action per day, until you achieve your desired big dreams.

Let's say you want to make 1,000,000 in one year, and you are offering a value for 1,000.
One year is 365 days, with 1,000 worth of value, you need 1000 people to offer the value.

Therefore, you can divide 1,000 sales by 356 days = 2.76, approximately 3 sales per day.
That means, if you can try to sell 3 values (products or services) per day, in One Year, you will have sold about 1,095 sales.

You can see now that it's easier and less overwhelming, instead of focusing on selling to 1,000 people in one year, your focus is now how to try and sell 2-3 value (products or services) per day, you can see that is a lesser work to do.

CHAPTER FIVE
THE PRIZE OF SUCCESS

The Prize of success is paid in advance, you don't get success first and pay the prize later.

For farmers to Harvest Fruits, first, they have to plant some seeds, then they have to water and weed them, and they have to have patience until harvest time.

Most people today, wish to become successful or be a millionaire, you don't need a superpower or brain to become successful and rich, all you need is the right knowledge (the truth), actions, and patients. In fact, those who are successful and rich don't have two heads, they just discover some secret or principles that work, and they act upon it.

Some people are not actually successful not because they don't have the knowledge or take action but because they did not exercise enough patients till harvest time, some don't water and weed their farms, and because of this, either there is nothing to harvest or fewer things to harvest.

To be a millionaire, you must understand the principle of success, just like the farmer that sows seeds, water, and weed the farm and has patience until harvest time, the same thing is applicable to any type of business you want to start today.

To become successful like the farmer, there are sowing and harvest time, when you create or offer your product or service, you must water and weed it, meaning; you have to market and promote it, you must let it reach more people, you must get feedbacks on how to improve your product or service, learn a better way to deliver them, better way to sell them, etc, have patient, keep on doing what you are doing, exercise patient until harvest time, when your product or service will hit your desire goals, generate millions and billions of money for you.

CHAPTER SIX

VALUE

What is a Value?

Value can refer to something (product or service) that can add value (improvement, enhancement, etc) to someone's life or business.

A value can be informed of a Product or Service.

For example, I'm an Author, Graphic Designer, Developer, etc.

I'm an Author because I write books and a book can be categorised as a Product, be it in Digital or Physical form.
I'm also a Web & Mobile Apps Developer, meaning that I can help individuals or businesses to design and build web or mobile apps, develop Software, etc; the kind of value can be categorized as a service.

Either way, I'm offering value to these individuals and businesses either as products (books, digital courses, etc,) or services to help them improve or enhance their lives and businesses.

As you read my book(s), it will help you to improve your life and increase your knowledge and understanding.

You can create or offer your own products or services, or you can also offer other people or businesses products or services, in return for some wages or commissions.

Note that it's not compulsory, you create your own product or service, if you can't create your own, you can start with other people's or businesses' products or services, maybe as a direct sales, working with them in their businesses, then later you can create your own products or services.

If you are starting new or afresh, I will advise you to look for good products or services that lots of people are looking for and partner with the owner to help them make sales and get your own commission percentage after sales.

If you want to create your own product or service, there are many products or services you can create or offer.

- We have Digital and Physical Products
- Physical products require lots of money to create, can also look for manufacturers in china or India to help you.
- Digital products are easier and less costly to produce.

Type of Digital Product you can products you can produce

- Documents
- Online Courses
- Video
- Audio
- Music
- Graphics
- Photography
- Ebooks
- Software
- Applications

Services
To offer your own services, you need to have or acquire some skills, if you have a skill already, you can use that, example like writing a blog post, if you are good at writing a blog post, you can convert them to ebooks, if you can design graphics or website, you can start offering a service.

From experience, you can sell more products and services, why? Because, it takes less time to produce a product, but for services, you need more time to deliver each services orders you sell, you will be trading time for money.

Nevertheless, you can employ more people to help deliver your services.

To sell more products or services, you will need more hands (I.e more people) to help you sell more, faster, and reach more people.

CHAPTER SEVEN

SKILLS

You are not a millionaire yet, because you don't have the skills required to become a millionaire.
Becoming a millionaire is a skill of its own that will need to learn.

This book will help you do so. All you have to do is to read, meditate and take action about the knowledge you will learn from this book, and the rest will be history.

To be able to generate some wealth that your heart desired, you definitely need some skills.

As a person, you need at least one or more skills.
Below I will list some skills that you will need to achieve some success.

- Book Writing
- Graphic Design
- Website design
- Public speaking
- Web and mobile app develop
- Fashion design
- Video editing
- Leadership skill
- Management silks
- Financial and investment skills
- Interior decoration
- Baking and catering skills
- Hotel management skills
- Sales, promotion & marketing skills
- Etc

The list can go on and on.

The truth of the matter is that you need some skills to make more.

If you want to create your own products or offer your own services, you need to acquire some skills to do this.
So I will advise that you go for skills that match your passion or talents.

For example, for someone like me, I'm good at almost anything technical and I also love drawing. My talent (technical) and passion (design), have led me to acquire Graphic Designing skill, my technical talent have also help learn how to write programming languages to develop web and mobile apps. I also like to share my knowledge, and this passion for sharing knowledge has made me be interested in writing a book, creating an online course, and training students.

Whatever you love doing or have fun doing, can be your talent or passion, your job is to find skills that match with them, then learn them and start making money with them.

CHAPTER EIGHT

ABILITY TO SELL

The number one skill anyone must have to succeed in life is the ability to sell, if you don't have any other skills but you can see, you will never lack money or are poor.

In fact, from childhood, we have been selling, when we are hungry, we cry, when we need something, we cry, when we want the relationship we negotiate for it, and so on and so forth.

Selling is the most avoidable career most people will not want to venture into.

But if you can try to learn how to sell, you will definitely become successful if you sell the good and right products or services that can change lots of people's lives.

This book, will not cover sales training, but I will advise you to enroll in a Sales and Marketing Course so that you can learn more and a better way to sell.

I will recommend Brian Tracy Sales Training and course, you can also enroll for one-on-one classes in your local area.

If you know how to sell already, then the journey is much easier.

With technology, selling is much much easier, you can create your own online stores (eCommerce), and you can use Facebook, Instagram, Twitter, YouTube, Amazon, etc to sell your products or services.

Your job is to take some courses or training that will teach you deeper on how to use the online platform to generate sales.

I'm also recommending my Course: 365 days Success Challenge (Zero to Hero)

Where I will be covering some skill acquisition courses on:
- Book Writing

- Public Speaking
- Sales Skills
- Digital Marketing (Facebook, Email Marketing, etc)
- eCommerce Setup and Payment Integration
- Etc

You can Pre-Order Now!
https://israeljoshua.com.ng/index.php/courses/365-days-success-challenge-zero-to-hero-course

CHAPTER NINE
CONTACTS AND NETWORKS

Every wealth-creation ingredient is based on the following part:
Value (Product & Services) & People (Customers)

The more people know you and trust you, the better you can sell to them anything.
Meaning the more contacts you have, the more you can sell.

People will not buy from you if they don't first know you, then trust you.
It's very hard to sell something to a stranger, which knows as COLD CALLING OR COLD SELLING.

So to become more successful, you need to reach more people, build more trust and build more contact databases or do some network.

These days, it is just easier to build contacts and a fan base, using social media, you can build followers and subscribers, by posting useful, educated, expert tips and entertainment content to gain more followers and subscribers.
That way you can reach more people build more trust and be able to sell to them any Paid or Premium content, products, or services.

Your job is to start now building trusted content, networks, followers, or subscribers.

LEVERAGE AND PARTNERSHIP
Building trusted contacts or networking to reach more people and gain their trust, takes lots of time, maybe within 6 months to 5 years or more.

You may not have the luxury of time to do so, as you may want to start making money immediately.

You can jump-start your success by leveraging other people's contacts or databases.

Most people and brands have built lots of fanbase and subscribers on social media platforms, ships, and retail and have built many trusted shoppers and customers base over the course of the years, you can leverage these fans or customers base to sell your products or services. All you have to do is to reach out to them, you can partner with their base on some percentage commission or any other relevant agreement your may work out with them.

You can also leverage some affiliate networking websites or companions to help you push your products or services to their affiliate networking database.

Don't be greedy about making money, you can't make money alone faster yourself when other people make money by selling your products or services for you, because you are leveraging on their time and customers base, you will have some free time and be stress-free.

Millionaires don't make money by selling all their products or services themselves.
So go and search for people or businesses that will partner with you and go to work, let them make money for you, while they too make money for themselves.

You can also hire or build your sales team, if your aim is to build a company, this way, you are leveraging on your staff or team time in exchange for money.

CHAPTER TEN
TWO-EDGED SWORD THAT BREAKS YOU THROUGH ONLINE SUCCESS

Every online platform that is super successful today is using these strategies called: 2-Edged-Sword. Meaning:
- · Free Offer
- · Paid Offer

Free Offer, helps you to attract lots of people.
For example, Facebook offers free signup, google offers free gmail (email), Amazon(Kindle, etc) offers free signup to upload books, products, etc, and no money is paid upfront.

These methods of online business strategies have made most online platforms that you can think of becoming more successful than ever.

So you too can tap into this strategy, you can offer part of your products or services for free, that way, it will attract more people or customers to your business.

For example, I'm giving out some free chapters (free version) of this book for free.
This strategy is a win-win strategy, I give them free chapters of my book, and in return, they input their name, email, WhatsApp number (optional), country (optional), etc., and they agreed that I can send them updates, sales promotion news, etc.
That way, I can reach them later, and I can persuade them to buy the full book later if the free version they downloaded looks promising that they will get more and better knowledge by getting the full book. I can also send them weekly or monthly updates, etc.

Paid Offers, can be in different formats, some membership can ask you to upgrade from free to premium packages, so that you can enjoy more premium features, some platforms like Facebook, Instagram, Twitter, and google/YouTube can make money through Advertising, or opting for premium features, website like Amazon (kindle, etc) and other eCommerce platform makes money through commission each time the products or services you uploaded on their platform generate sales.

Like this book, I'm using these two formats to sell my book:
- Download Free Chapters (Free Version)
- Order Full book

Those who have not read my previous books before can first download my free version, when they read it and got some confidence, they may decide to pay for the full book.

Some people who have trust in my book and others can decide to buy my book at once, it all depends on choices.

CHAPTER ELEVEN
YOU NEED MONEY TO MAKE MORE MONEY

Most people want to make money without any money invested in advance, it's just like a farmer, you you don't sow a seed, how do you expect to harvest fruits, it's not possible.

Every successful people or business, at one time or another, needs some money and used the money to multiply more money, the money you invested upfront in your products or services is the seeds you sow in advance of your business success.

Buying this book, for example, the money you used is an investment upfront you invested to become a millionaire.

To start a business, or sell a product or service, you will need money at one point or the other to boost your way through.

For example, you will need money for one or more of the followings:
- Money to produce your first prototype
- Money for production or mass production
- Money for marketing, promotion, or advertisement
- Money to deliver products or services
- Etc

Of course, when you are starting afresh, most often, you won't have enough money to get started.
So don't be afraid to ask for help, if you don't have enough money to start your new business idea.

The best place to start is with family and friends, all you have to do is sell them, your vision and dreams, and assure them that your vision and dream are great and it will work, and you can motivate them that they will get interested in their money or the will get shares in your business if the money you are requesting from them is huge.

Your ability to convince them to give your their hard-earned money will be determined if they will give your their money.

If you have some successful and rich people in your family, don't be afraid to approach them, most importantly, you must be a person that is trusted and worthy, a man of his word, and a person of good character.
All you have to do, is to strongly tell them about your vision and dreams, about your idea, and how this is going to make positive differences and improve people's lives.

If you can get your prototype or sample ready, you can approach private or public investors, to put their money into your business idea.

Money is important at one point in your business, you will need to promote, market, or advertise your idea or business, most people spend tons of money on producing their products or services, but spend less money promoting, marketing, or advertising their products or services.

Most people or business fails not because their products or services are not good, but because they refused or ignorantly didn't invest enough money into their marketing, promoting, or advertising campaigns. Selling is about numbers, the more people you can reach, the better you can sell your products or services, and you can speed up your sales by reaching more people that needed your products or service through your marketing, promotion, or advertising.

Don't wait until you can generate some money yourself, you may wait forever, and other people or businesses may start that your same or similar idea or business and push you out of the business. So it's important that you find a way to secure some money needed for you to quickly start production fast, and sell your idea, product, or service.

There are no millionaires or billionaires out there who have not used other people's money to make more money for themselves and the people that borrowed that money.

CHAPTER TWELVE
HOW I MADE N1,095,000 (MILLION) IN ONE YEAR
(Bonus Chapter)

In this book, I will show my experience of how I made N1,095,000 in one year selling my ebook.

You will also learn one or two things if you are ready in selling some kind of product or service online.

Remember, the story of the farmer you read in my previous chapter, that story applies to every successful life, patient is the reason why most people are not successful the way they actually wanted to be.

First, I was not in a rush to make this money, I understand the principle:
- The law of sowing and reaping.
- Focus on one goal until is accomplished.
- Concentrate solely on one thing, until it's done.
- Be Consistent with your goals and don't jump around.
- Be Patient, learn, correct, grow, etc.

I understand the principle of sowing and reaping, I know that if I sow, I must reap, I also know that if I sow good seed and focus, concentrate, and be consistent (weed and water my plant) with time and patient; my harvest time will come.

So my plan was very simple.
I use Facebook ads, my blog website (israeljoshua.com.ng) other platforms like; solar & kindle, flutterwave for payment, to sell my ebook.

Sow: I used a Facebook ad, and pay Facebook N600 every day, with N600 Facebook ad, by focusing and concentrating, I keep on doing this for about 1 year, while I still have other products (ebooks & courses) advertising on Facebook. I do not tamper with this particular ebook but I stayed consistent with patience.

Of course, at first, there were no sales, later after people have seen my ad several times and because I didn't quit showing them the ebook ad, some people start developing an interest, so have also downloaded my free chapter and found interest in getting the full book, so few sales start coming in, later in few months, at least I sell 2-3 books or more per day.

And those that have read my book, are still seeing my ads and they start commenting about how good my book is, and these help more people to trust the book and decide to buy my book.

Up till now, the Facebook adverts are still on, if the ad continues to give me 2-3 sales per day, I will still continue to do that.

So below, let's do the millions maths:

- ✓ **With the average of 3 sales per day = N1,200 x 3 = N3,600**
- ✓ **N600 Ad budget per day = N3,600 sales - N600 ad = N3,000 profit per day**
- ✓ **Times the daily profits for 1 year which is 365days**
- ✓ **N3,000 profit x 365days = N1,095,000 / year**

You can see that patience is the key if you promote any product or service that you know lots of people will like in 14 to 30 days, and you didn't make any sales, you should stop, but until then keep on trying.

The only possible reason why people are not buying, maybe because they are not clear enough what the benefits or values your product or service will deliver to them, you can create about 5 different ads/copywriter and try them all to see which attract more likes, comments, and clicks, you can change the title of the book, if you are selling book, you alter your ad heading, graphic design or the photo you are using, test and test until you see the one that flies, then you can concentrate on that and run the ads for at least 14-30days, if it works and generates sales for you, you focus solely on that ad until it stops working.

www.ingramcontent.com/pod-product-compliance
Lightning Source LLC
Chambersburg PA
CBHW050324220526
45465CB00005B/2123